USAJOBS

A Guide to Understanding the Federal Government Hiring Process

Sherron J. Moore

USAJOBS: A GUIDE TO UNDERSTANDING THE FEDERAL GOVERNMENT HIRING PROCESS

Copyright © 2022 by SHERRON J. MOORE

ISBN: 979-8-9869100-0-0

All rights reserved. No part of this publication may be reproduced, distributed, or transmitted in any form or by any means, including photocopying, recording, or other electronic or mechanical methods, without the prior written permission of the publisher or author, except in the case of brief quotations embodied in critical reviews and certain other noncommercial uses permitted by copyright law.

Although every precaution has been taken to verify the accuracy of the information contained herein, the author and publisher assume no responsibility for any errors or omissions. No liability is assumed for damages that may result from the use of information contained within.

Dedication

God

My Mother – Gloria Moore

My Father – Eugene Moore, Jr.

My Grandmom – Earlean Moore

My Brother – Shareef Moore

My Nieces – Shariyah Moore and Samiyah Moore

My High School English Teacher- Beverly Trimboli

My Family and Friends

In loving memory of Eugene Moore, Eva Banks, and Earnestine Banks

Introduction

This guidebook will help you understand the federal government hiring process and will be a vital tool in your career path. You will learn the necessary steps of writing a winning resume, submitting your application, answering multiple types of questionnaires, preparing for your interview, and accepting the job offer.

Finally, you'll use this book as a key to open doors to a federal government position. This book will also help ease your frustrations when applying for job vacancies. In the meantime, always continue to build your resume with knowledge, experience, and skills.

Table of Contents

Navigating USAJOBS 6

Writing a Qualified Resume 7

Searching for Careers 11

Applying to Multiple Types of Questionnaires 13

Submitting Your Application 16

Becoming an Eligible and Referred Applicant 20

The Interview Process 23

Accepting the Best Job Offer 29

Words of Encouragement 31

Navigating USAJOBS

USAJOBS is the official federal government job site. By logging on to www.usajobs.gov you will be able to search for all federal jobs, create multiple resumes, apply for jobs, and check your application status. The system will also email you job notifications that interest you. The more you job search on USAJOBS, the more the site will become familiar to you. Announcements will become easier to read, questionnaires will be less difficult to answer, and navigating the site will become second nature in your daily routine.

Writing a Qualified Resume

Start by initiating an account and profile in USAJOBS. Creating a resume format is optional, but it is the preferred format to use by human resources officials. A cover letter is not required or needed for a government job. USAJOBS resume format includes your contact information, desired location, veteran information, job duties, references, certifications, education, awards, and training courses.

First list your present employer or the last employer detailing all job duties and responsibilities that you performed. No job duty is too small or too big to list on your resume. Include every task, whether it was assigned or unassigned by your manager and staff members. Also, include your experience and accomplishments that relate to the job you're applying for. You want to make sure the information in your resume is relevant to prospective employers, focusing on the skills and experience needed to perform the job. Keep the job duties that are relevant to the position towards the top of your resume. Remember to give as many specific examples as possible in parentheses throughout your resume. Tailor it to each job that you plan to apply for. You may want to have on file more than one USAJOBS resume and/or switch your job duties around when you apply for each job. At the same time, make sure your resume doesn't look crowded and there aren't any gaps in dates of employment. There is no universal resume format, only guidelines, and recommendations.

Actively sell your qualifications by focusing on accomplishments and results. Resumes should be a concise and factual listing of your education, experience, and accomplishments. Make sure you have no gaps in employment in your resume if possible. USAJOBS resumes usually average around four to five pages. Using strong action verbs, concrete nouns, and being descriptive will demonstrate the qualities you possess, setting your resume aside from others. Your resume should demonstrate and reflect your qualifications for the position you're applying for. Formatting your resume in bullet points is always best because it's organized and easy to read. Use concise phrases and clauses rather than complete sentences.

Share as many supporting details as possible. Use parenthesis to include examples of how you performed your job duties. Doing this makes it easier for the manager to review how qualified you are. Be very clear when writing your resume and avoid using acronyms. The resume size font should be either 10 or 12 points. It is best to use font types such as Times New Roman, Arial, and Verdana because it's easier on the reader's eyes. Always keep your font size and font style consistent throughout your resume. As a suggestion, use black ink on ivory resume paper for a professional appearance. Lastly, keep a separate list of references available upon request. Remember, your resume is only a door opener. Your goal is to obtain a personal interview.

Searching for Careers

USAJOBS permits you to search by agency, salary, occupation location, and grade.

Using multiple grade levels allows you to have broader search results. Searching by a specific agency narrows your search results. A vital strategy for finding a government job is to search daily or search every other day. It is best to set a reminder on your calendar to log onto the USAJOBS website until it becomes second nature to you. My favorite step in searching for jobs on USAJOBS is to search by multiple GS Levels simultaneously. Job announcements with few or many vacancies give you a better chance of getting an interview and ultimately being offered the position. You still want to apply for announcements with one vacancy. You never know if you possess the necessary experience/education that the agencies are requiring to fulfill their vacancy announcement.

Finally, it's a good idea to search for different series of jobs. You never know what career path may interest you and/or what job you may be highly qualified for. Before applying, always check the status of the position, which are permanent, part-time, internship, temporary, and seasonal. Many agencies post temporary jobs. It's worthwhile for a person who is not working to get his or her foot in the door of the federal government by applying for temporary and seasonal jobs. Oftentimes, if there is enough money in the budget of that department, the agency will bring the employee on full-time or encourage him or her to apply for a permanent position. You can also create up to five resumes and save job searches to receive automatic notifications to your personal email account for when specific jobs become available. In addition, the system allows you to revise, delete, or save jobs that you wish to review later.

Applying to Multiple Types of Questionnaires

You'll notice there are multiple types of questionnaire formats on USAJOBS. Applying these questionnaires takes time. Human Resources officials have the option of selecting which format they prefer to use for each vacancy. Below are some examples of the kinds of questionnaires:

Task-Based Questionnaires – Task-based statements are most often used as questionnaires. In this type of questionnaire, a statement is listed and then followed by choices (A-E) where you would check off your level and/or knowledge of each job task. Be careful when selecting answer (E) because that is usually an expert statement. Many agencies know that applicants always select (E) to rate themselves as an expert. Agencies will check resumes thoroughly to see if they have demonstrated expert experience and knowledge of work duties. Some agencies will even ask for a list of employment, job title, and dates of employment in the questionnaire sections. Other agencies will switch up (A-E) statements because they know applicants sometimes do not read statements and automatically select option (E) as their answers.

Competency-Based Questionnaires - Competency-based questionnaires are questions that determine your level of experience. The statements usually range from no experience to supervised experience.

Minimum Qualification Questionnaires - Minimum qualification questionnaires are set up to easily screen applicants out of the process. There are usually only two options to choose from: option A or B. These questionnaires are often used for wage grade vacancies because it's easier to screen applicants.

Many announcements contain a link where you can review the questions before you apply. It would be in your best interest and to your advantage to review the questions before applying for the position.

Submitting Your Application

Please remember the supporting documents section is very important. I highly recommend that you apply online and do not fax any documents, as it can take a couple of days until your faxed documents are uploaded. Please be aware if one document is missing, you will be disqualified and found ineligible for the job. Agencies will not contact you for missing documents because they have hundreds of resumes to review.

Do not forget to include the below-supporting documents:

1. **Your Resume**
2. **Veteran Documents (DD-214, SF-15, and/or Disability Letter)**

3. *Transcripts*

4. *Awards, Certificates, and/or Licenses*

5. *Typing Skills Certification Statement*

My advice for veterans is to always make sure that all your supporting documents are included with the application to receive all additional points for the open vacancy announcement. By law, veterans preference gives eligible veterans an advantage over many other applicants. Veterans preference recognizes citizens who have suffered economic loss by serving their country, acknowledging the obligation owed to disabled veterans.

Not all veterans receive five to ten points added to their resumes. Points are based upon their creditable duty of service. If you are a spouse or a widow of a veteran, please make sure you submit the required documents as well. It is noteworthy to know that non-veterans often receive notification letters informing them that a sufficient number of veterans applied. Please do not let these types of notifications discourage you from applying for the position you are interested in.

Most jobs close five days from the date posted. If possible, apply once you see the open vacancy announcement. Also, save jobs when you see them in case you cannot apply at that exact moment. Please make sure you answered all the questions and double-check your answers. Make sure all supporting documents are uploaded. Under the job duties section, remember to list as many job duties as possible from previous and/or current jobs. Again, it is important to keep the relevant job duties for each specific job towards the top of each job listed on your resume. Most importantly, please ensure that all sections of your application are completed.

Before submitting your application, verify that all your contact information is correct and current, including your address, phone number, and email address. You don't want to miss out on any phone calls or emails. Finally, print out each job announcement, your answers, and the resume you submitted for each job. You can change your answers and upload documents before the announcement closes. After the announcement closes, no changes can be made.

Again, make sure every section is completed. Nothing is left blank! There are no right or wrong answers to the questionnaires. Being honest is best when answering all questions. Human Resources officials usually will compare your questionnaire to your resume. You don't want to get caught falsifying your resume. Resumes that are falsified will be forwarded to OPM (Office of Personnel Management) for further review.

Becoming an Eligible and Referred Applicant

The initial process can take up to six weeks to know if you are found eligible and/or referred. It is important to remember that the total process of being found eligible, referred, and selected can take up to three months from the closing date of the announcement. The qualification section of the vacancy announcement breaks down how you will be found eligible. You must possess the job duties and/or knowledge of job duties to be found qualified, eligible, and/or referred to selecting officials. The duties and skills that you've previously or currently performing must be found in your resume. Be sure to be honest and give yourself the best rating based on your experience and/or education.

In all announcements, you will see the terms "general experienced and/or specialized experience" required for the job position. General experience is better known as beginner skills and basic skill sets. General experience progressively shows you can perform the job being announced. Specialized experience is specific skill sets and/or more advanced levels of skills. This kind of experience is usually obtained in a position like the job being announced. Read carefully what type of skills, experience, and/or knowledge are needed for every job position. For some jobs, you can qualify for both education and experience. For some jobs, you can qualify on experience only. My advice for rating yourself for education and/or experience is as follows:

1. ***If you have obtained a degree, experience, superior academic achievement (GPA 3.0 or higher), and/or belong to an Honor Society, rate yourself for all.***

2. *If you have obtained experience only, rate yourself only for the experience.*

3. *If you have obtained a degree and no experience, then rate yourself for only education.*

The Interview Process

Always dress in a business and professional manner by wearing preferably dark colors. Make eye contact with all interviewers and greet everyone that you encounter at the agency on the day of your interview. You never know who will be observing you, so be polite, and professional, speak clearly, and remain calm. Always bring three or more copies of your resume on professional resume paper. You don't need to carry awards, certificates, transcripts, or a cover letter because the human resources official will have already reviewed your documents. Interviewers may not ask in-depth questions about what you know about their agency and/or department, but you should be apprised of their agency. I have found that interviewers tend to ask more situational questions in which you must give examples from your previous jobs.

Below are sample interview questions:

1. Tell me about yourself?

2. What do you know about this company or organization?

3. What are your biggest strengths?

4. What are your weaknesses?

5. What are you looking for in a new position?

6. Where do you see yourself in the next 5 years?

7. How do you prioritize your work?

8. How do you deal with pressure or a stressful situation?

9. Give an example of how you have handled a challenge in the workplace before?

10. Give an example of when you showed leadership qualities?

Prepare good interview questions about the agency and/or job in which you are interviewing. By asking the interviewer questions, you show that you have prepared for the interview as well as your interest in the position. Simply, pick a few questions that you think best fit your needs. Don't overload the employer with questions but remember that you are being evaluated for your insightfulness.

Here are examples of questions you can ask:

1. ***Where do you foresee the future of your agency?***
2. ***Can you describe your management and/or work style?***
3. ***Can you describe a typical day in this position?***
4. ***How is your department organized and how are your teams arranged?***

5. *What are the prospects for growth and advancement in your department and/or agency?*
6. *How does a person advance in your agency?*
7. *What are some challenges and obstacles that I may encounter in this position?*
8. *What can I expect walking into this job?*
9. *Will there be any formal or informational training?*
10. *What are the next steps in the interview process?*

Always end the interview with, "What are the next steps in the interview process" and reiterate why you are still interested in the position based on your experience, skills, and career path. Explain why the position is parallel to your career path and how you can be an asset to the organization. Interviewers tend to focus on your current and/or past experiences relating to the vacancy announcement. They will ask you to give many examples of how you performed a particular job duty and/or how you would perform a specific task. You may be asked to describe programs, situations, challenges, and/or obstacles. Please be honest when answering the questionnaires because some agencies will ask how you specifically performed your job duties.

Per federal government policies and procedures, human resources officials should send out disposition letters. However, some officials don't complete the necessary steps to let you know if you are found eligible and/or referred to the selecting official for the job. My advice is not to constantly call agencies to check your job status. Although, if you decide to call an agency, call once or twice after one or two months. Remember, agencies have 90 to 120 days to select candidates. Give as many professional references as possible. From my experience, you will not be penalized if you say, "Do not contact my manager," or "Contact me first." A good number of professional references to have is four, just in case, they cannot reach one or two individuals. In most cases, agencies contact your references and employers that you have listed before a job offer is extended to you.

Accepting the Best Job Offer

If possible, my advice is to negotiate a salary after projecting a justifiable means of living. Once a final offer letter has been granted, changes may be unavailable. Always ask pertinent questions before accepting a job offer to get the highest-paid salary. The following are good questions to ask the hiring official:

1. Is the current salary negotiable?
2. Will relocation expenses be covered?
3. Will you offer a bonus incentive?

Many government agencies have potential promotion growth within their agencies. I highly recommend that you ask around and do research on what agencies you wish to pursue a career in. Ask the agency if the position has quotas that must be met consistently, periodically, or not at all. In my opinion, your goal should be to work for an agency where there is growth, advancement, and employee incentives. I have found that it's important to feel valued by an employer. Often it is listed in the vacancy announcement if relocation expenses will be covered. If relocation expenses are not listed as covered, then definitely inquire about potentially being able to negotiate this. In some cases, government agencies will pay for relocation expenses, especially if they want you to accept a job offer.

Words of Encouragement

In conclusion, commit yourself to searching for a position on USAJOBS at least every other day. New announcements become available daily. Practice and implement these steps into your job search. Always be persistent, determined, and open-minded.

www.ingramcontent.com/pod-product-compliance
Lightning Source LLC
Chambersburg PA
CBHW070654100426
42734CB00048B/2991